"You have just now understood that all sentient beings

have already attained Buddhahood.

The world of life and death

and the world of nirvana are like a dream."

Mugai Nyodai

QUEER
HAIKU

"Queer wasn't originally an inclusive umbrella term.
It means 'different' / 'weird' and we grew up in that era.
We were gay. We took back the words 'Faggot' and 'Queer'.
It was for us, the gays who rejected the sanitized image.
We were a clique like any other. We gatekept like any subculture.
We were the Brotherhood of Mutants. We didn't want to conform.
We didn't feel shame, nor wanted to live within the status quo.
We wanted to live on our terms, without any regrets.
not corporate-friendly lives on the cover of The Advocate."

R.A. Lopez

This Book is Dedicated to

Nanaki, who has moved heaven and earth for me

Dad, who gave me the ultimate power

Mom, an often distant star of love

Grandma, who has always secretly told me I'm her favorite

Grandpa Burt, who taught me the meaning of being a man

Valentina, for providing momentum and a kindred soul

Jonathan, for the lovely artwork and over a decade of friendship

Luna, for lighting the way and being my beacon

Spirits, all those who have left, you know who you are

Tiny Tina, who eternally hunts the Grassy Plains for purple buffalo

Table of Contents

Book I : Book of Blood

The Book of Blood explores the relationships between us.

Book II : Book of Bone

The Book of Bone muses on the world we are anchored to.

Book III : Book of Flesh

The Book of Flesh is unapologetically erotic, adult, and taboo.

~

This book is divided into three thematic sub books
based upon the three physical elements of Darkness.

Often Zen is achieved in a state
of 'no mind' or 'nothingness'.

BOOK I : BOOK OF BLOOD

FALSE

first he said one thing
i drew within his red lines
yet he still walks off

MISSING YOU

i feel so alone
i wish he was next to me
i can't sleep.. he's gone

HOPE

something special sparked
light appears as the clouds part
my heart's fire alight

TORNADO

it was all a blur
it all happened so damn fast
our whirlwind romance

WORRY

i still haven't heard
call and call but it just rings
where could you have gone

DISTANCE

only a few hours
a true test for our future
don't give up on us

LDR

two hearts beat as one
hours on the phone just laughing
he touches my soul

HOPE

something special sparked
light appears as the clouds part
feelings can't be wrong

ICE

his hands are so cold
freezing just like his blue eyes
he'll never know me

HAUNTING

that faded picture
makes me remember things lost
you are like a ghost

ROBOT

cash fused to his brain
electronic impulses
boy toy battery

AWE

dreaming beautiful
moonbeams dance over his form
venus as a boy

ACTOR

undefined beauty
between silver screens he steps
solid gold closet door

COMPETITION

next to me he flirts
the other guy looks jealous
i'm really confused

FLAKE

tonight is the night
i'm here but no sign of him
fuck i got stood up

PAINT

adjectives describe
the details are essential
words colour the world

IDENTITY

whats in a title
rose by any other name
i label myself

MISMATCH

plaid on stripes six shades
belt hair shoes socks do not match
god he is so straight

TIPSY

bubbly in my glass
my throat burns from elixir
the room moves with me

HOODIE

blonde hair and blue eyes
goofy smile my boy next door
fireworks and ice cream

TARANTULA

lanky gothic geek
so much potential unbound
my loving spider

STARVING

so hungry within
my heart is like a deep grave
fill me with your love

BOI

he's so very soft
not girly just sensitive
i need to hold him

POCKET SIZED

short cute and spunky
he has more hair than he should
my little hobbit

FIRST SIGHT

my knee touches his
a shock a spark hearts ignite
eyes meet flames consume

TIES THAT BIND

treasure your bloodline
what's thicker? blood or water?
friends aren't forever

STANDARDS

so many offers
won't waste my time on randoms
don't ever settle

RIDICULOUS

six within the six
the seether is you
our paradise lost

SIX YEARS

across this country
we have felt and grown so much
the longest journey

BULLDOG CHIHUAHUA

one fat one skinny
opposites they play they bite
but they are equals

MELD

arms legs entangle
the beauty of completion
our own yin and yang

NANAKI

comic book bronx boy
angry loving jealous shy
be my spiderman

WHILE YOU SLEEP

call me dreamcatcher
i stand against the dark night
chasing the nightmares

TAKE CARE

take care with your words
sometimes it's your bark that bites
some things cross the line

ODAAT

waking up with you
life pulls us apart briefly
before we merge and meld

MY GREATEST FEAR

you will never know
until your heart is captured
the true fear of loss

FIREPLACE

let me be your fire
warm your chill bones and damp clothes
lust passion and strength

TOUCH

this is my language
i need it and i want it
my skin and your skin

PRIAPRISM

if your erection
continues after four hours
please call a doctor

SLEEVEHEART

a sensitive soul
beauty wonder tragedy
it all makes me cry

BOOK II : BOOK OF BONE

ME TIME

midnight toke moonlight
icy fingers trace my arm
sipping cold soda

NIGHT DRIVE

everything is packed
snacks and water stuff my bag
eight long ones to go

CITY LIGHTS

skyscrapers so high
a sea of lights float around
i thrive while they sleep

SILENT FAME

nobody knows me
when i step into the room
i am dangerous

CLEANING

break it up so fine
stems and seeds shall be removed
load the shake first please

JOINT

give me some zigzags
finger roll origami
why not roll two more

BREATHE

add fire free the smoke
puff puff and try not to choke
inhale exhale high

I LOVE MARY

red and purple hair
love is patient love is kind
sticky luscious jade

FIREFLY

flying will o' wisp
dancing and glowing within
soul of a lost child

STORMCLOUD

rumbling grumbling clouds
raindrops falling on my head
lightning will strike twice

CLEANSE

sponge and bodywash
scrub in all the right places
wash well and pat dry

SHOPGIRL

foundation lipstick
mascara and long lashes
how can I help you

SLOW MORNING

i am so damn tired
paralyzed monotony
someone please save me

DELIVERY

sausage and mushrooms
bubbly cheese and tangy sauce
ding dong cash or card

HAIKU

first five syllables
second line add seven more
then finish with five

SORE

scratching wheezing cough
my throat feels like sandpaper
my lungs on the floor

MOSQUITOS

flying carnivore
malicious vampires descend
stop sucking my blood

WINDOWS

the blue screen of death
illegal operation
ctrl alt delete

HELLO SANRIO

pink pretty kitty
notebooks candy hats pens mugs
japanese profits

LOVECRAFT

antiquarian
grotesque daemons in the dark
into the abyss

JAVA

drip.. sniff.. i am called
coffee my elixir now
i need my caffeine

CHIHUAHUA
small apple shaped head
eyes the size of bowling balls
no taco for you

IZMIR STINGER

i breathe in and out
that white smoke between my lips
respite from my life

NOSTALGIA

legend of zelda
thundercats and transformers
he-man and mario

COMMUNICATE

tell me what you mean
written verbal nonverbal
but mean what you say

BJORK

icelandic siren
mystery within her voice
she explains it all

TORI

these little earthquakes
faeries whisper wondrous tales
gold dust in our hands

PJ

sixty foot queenie
rivers desires monsters
just put on that dress

MATHEMATICS

numbers and fractions
equations on my paper
it doesn't add up

TELEMARKET

people calling us
they hate it and we hate it
but the phones still ring

BASIC

independent clause
subject verb a complete thought
a simple sentence

WORK SEARCH

round and round again
employees of corporate
turnover rates soar

M

kylie wannabe
a career thief pop star queen
blowjobs for votes fail

PROPHECY

six demons arise
ancient terror from beyond
not all hope is lost

SIGN UP

your information
enter data sign accept
download and install

SPOILED

i won't pay your bills
you don't even clean or cook
fuck these gold diggers

ARISE

dark creeping horror
the dead thing awoke down deep
pungent scent of death

DANCE WITH ME

let's get physical
move with me and groove with me
right down to the ground

NONSENSE

mongoose deergasm
fryboys and rusty buckets
toad oil with salad

CYCLE

everchanging world
show us your deepest oceans
time marches forward

LIFE

flowers in springtime
bloom slowly through their journey
life is beautiful

EVIL

whirlpools of darkness
the shades of ire swirl about
violence within

ADVISOR

fortune lies within
give me knowledge of my path
show my fate cookie

ECONOMY

man lives day to day
an endless dance of business
man is a machine

GLITTER

sell your soul for gold
man can't live on bread alone
this results in death

SPIT

my poetry flows
words dance in a carnivale
i forevermore

ANOTHER WORLD

why is the sky.. green?
the ground.. purple and orange?
and the water red!?

SAFE SPACES

social justice crap
ugh neo feminism
go fuck your third wave

CRITICAL

it stops on twenty
confirm success roll again
the damage doubles

MONDAYS

so hectic yet slow
the weekend vanished so quick
oh to be at home

ENCOUNTER

why the ugly look
snarling he calls me faggot
i won't stand for this

PISSED

fire within my veins
my heart beats for sweet revenge
hatred and fury

HIGH ROAD

i file the charges
rising up above his words
my head is held high

TENSION

my nerves are steel
electricity inside
the world will shudder

NIKE

the winged goddess
her halo of victory
don't ever give up

SEREPTICIA

majestic darkness
primal immortality
darkness perfection

APPRECIATION

time is so precious
gone like water down the drain
for each second counts

GLARE

bright flashes cut deep
sharp shimmering shards of light
i am without sight

CANON CANNON

that behemoth book
words that shake the earth through men
your faith is power

TUESDAY

the white flowers dance
spin in the breeze joyous wind
their petal party

SOUTH PARK FAGGOT

he rumbles past me
fat dude plus motorcycle
a pig on a hog

CLASSY

barbarian rogue
fighter cleric wizard bard
sorcerer druid

ROLES

what? top or bottom?
tank, healer, or D P S?
i just wanna play

POP KING

you pretty young thing
black white just leave me alone
false accusations

JEWELS

shining eternal
innocent but aged glory
rape our earth for gems

FRESA

that mexican bitch
designer knockoffs fools gold
you are fucking spoiled

SHOWERS

let the rain come down
chilled drops splash through my window
drip drop on my toes

MISCONCEPTIONS

warm thick smooth creamy
i'm talking about coffee
you're such a pervert

STRUGGLES

i lived on the streets
original fantastic
you're just a poseur

VENUS

buzz buzz on my lips
snap clap trap i close my mouth
crunch munch suppertime

LABOR

working all weekend
i'm not a slacker okay
but i need my time

INFRINGE

computer music
limewire napster utorrent
at the pirate bay

SITCOM MOM

only wants the best
giving and compromising
a bittersweet love

UNITY

flaming stars unite
one truth one light one justice
my heart swells with pride

VIEW

my mega meter
measure the distance between
i am so metric

MEDUSA

tangled nest, her crown
her eyes of stone eternal
serpentine empress

DREAM

rapid eye movement
visions of past and future
beyond the mind's eye

PAIN

shards of fire touch me
blood swells fear overtakes
lightning through my skill

GRAY

yin and yang balance
two halves of one become whole
chaos is quiet

FAITH

trust in what you feel
symbols idols and dogmas
i believe in me

EMPTY

nothingness inside
the black hole in existence
i was never here

TARDY

tick tock said the clock
late for an important date
i should just stay home

HONEY

sticky green so sweet
smoke thicker than red honey
fields of green i dream

BELMONT

my clan's destiny
protect the weak smite evil
our foe, Dracula

CHAI

cold crisp and with spice
touches of milk honey cloves
it cuddles my soul

OMELETTE

some salt and pepper
beat the eggs and splash with milk
fry flip serve with chives

SALAD

first slice the lettuce
drizzle with oil salt pepper
then top with croutons

SHRIMP COCKTAIL

peel the shrimp and boil
diced celery and sea salt
smother in shrimp sauce

HOLLANDAISE

two pots double boil
lemon butter and cayenne
egg yolks whisk swiftly

GRANDMA RICE

beef garlic cumin
tomato onion peppers
rice water simmer

LOPEZ STYLE FISH

splash fish with white wine
jalapenos butter salt
pinch of sugar broil

PUMPKIN

round fat and orange
cut me scoop me bake my seeds
light my soul within

BITCH LASAGNA

metameme with me
all your base belong to us
edgy feels for reals

THE EYE

silent conformist
wear the mask.. enter the dream..
big brother is here

ADVENTURE

when bored, remember
within every moment
you travel through time

EIGHTIES ETERNAL

nagel and neon
spandex and ankle warmers
the dream warriors

HUMAN

color gender creed
secularity beliefs
none of it matters

HUMAN > PERFECTION

tiles fit perfectly
people are not so lucky
imperfection zen

CORE

i see right through you
moving to the space between
and now i have you

PERSONA

my Jungian mask
slips between the archetypes
from my Velvet Room

SIN

man kills man for sport
red blood covers the pure hands
the cycle repeats

ENVY

the grass is greener
what i want is what you have
it is mine all mine

GLUTTONY

crunch munch slurp bite chew
eat all the bacon and eggs
cheese please then dessert

GREED

lobby to grease palms
rig scheme funnel wealth upwards
crushing wheels of debt

LUST

sex sells commonplace
we are slaves to curves flesh musk
blind yourself in awe

PRIDE

so where is the line
between vanity and pride
it's humility

SLOTH

it's not laziness
i'm seduced by the pleasure
roll around silk sheets

WRATH

i live by the sword
we destroy those we love most
give in lose control

VIRTUE

the ending can change
humans write their own story
be better than me

CHASTITY (VS LUST)

delayed gratification
you get me closer to god
let the right one in

ABSTINENCE (VS GLUTTONY)

sometimes less is more
moderation is key
even pigs can drown

ZEAL (VS SLOTH)

cherish every morning
you may never have been born
embrace each new day

LIBERALITY (VS GREED)

plates only hold so much
there's nothing wrong with success
you can't take it all with you

KINDNESS (VS ENVY)

we all can feel pain
one smile one call one minute
can change someone's life

HUMILITY (VS PRIDE)

no one is perfect
we all fall but that is life
humble pie is king

PATIENCE (VS WRATH)

change your perspective
what is done can't be undone
time can heal all wounds

ELEMENTS OF BALANCE

earth wind water fire
lightning and ice make six
these are the balance

ELEMENTS OF LIFE

sun moon and stars light
decay hate and shadow dark
this eternal struggle

LIGHT TRIAD

sun the love you give
moon the love reflected back
stars the love for all

DARK TRIAD

decay rots the mind
hate tortures and twists the heart
shadow corrupts soul

BOOK III : BOOK OF FLESH

SALESBOY

he sees me he smiles
shy and sweet honeysuckle
warm conversation

THREESOME

one bedroom three guys
grope grind kiss lick suck fuck shoot
aura afterglow

SIZE QUEEN

i am gonna choke
massive pillar of man meat
suppress gag reflex

TURTLENECK

short spiky black hair
tight clothing clings to his form
big nose means big dick

WEREWOLF

little black goatee
intelligent confident
short slim yet quite strong

GREASEMONKEY

his thick metal shaft
he slides it out of his bag
what does this look like

NOTHING BUT NECK

i feel it building
pearl drops glisten on your skin
he shoots and he scores

ROXXORZ

hot boy the rock boy
play your guitar just for me
set our spirits free

FUNCTION

i must generate
you and I must gyrate
our hips will now vibrate

NICE VIEW

unwrap his package
bulging from his khaki shorts
my tongue finds heaven

HONEY BUNS

two living bubbles
covered in that denim bliss
squeeze grab slap and pinch

MEERKAT

he smiles back smugly
i smack that cute little ass
then slide in behind

AFTERSCHOOL FUN

latchkey empty home
i hug him tight from behind
my hand slides down south

BISEXUAL

confusion inside
so don't come around here boy
just do what you want

PREPARATION

ankles in the air
i push forward within you
ouch we need more lube

STUDHORSE

dirty cowboy hat
those tight jeans make me wonder
come here wrangler butt

PHEREMOANS

sweat and cinnamon
tickles my nose my nuts twitch
i can smell his sex

MUSCLE

it's hard like a rock
the color of hazelnuts
worship those biceps

MASTURBATION

jerk jack whack pull stroke
rub your rod and beat that meat
shoot that hot load stud

JUST DESSERTS

suck my candy bar
melt in your mouth not your hand
sweet cream on your tongue

COOLIE

black hair and dark eyes
sensitive but masculine
god damn he's so hot

ANTICIPATION

my palms are sweaty
butterflies in my stomach
i can't bear the wait

NERD

a boy with glasses
he knows how to make me laugh
wrap my heart in his

CRUCIFIED

he is inside me
my navel runneth over
receive his pure seed

CONNECTION

i'm not a bottom
but i needed him inside
he fused into me

THUNDERCAT

he's like a kitten
he likes to purr scratch and bite
curl up nap time mew

LUBE

he grabs the jelly
he plays with his hole i watch
i enter he groans

BAD BOY

some guys play so tough
cocky and macho, so rough
soft skin within stone

LEGS

his tight hairy calves
his quadriceps flex and tease
i love men in shorts

HALLWAY ROYALTY

he looks like dean cain
perfect hair such a stud
take me superboy

BADUNKADUNK

his big ol booty
knocking people to the side
that ass clears the way

NEXT CHAIR

beside me stretching
treasure trail low boxer band
he basks in my lust

SYNTH

red lights handsome face
hot streets hot sheets and hot beats
sucks fucks where's my smokes

SHADOWS

kissing in the dark
see nothing feel everything
passion in darkness

FETISH

boys and their glasses
i can't help but stop and stare
my geek obsession

RIM

hairy buns so firm
his legs go up i see pink
lick his musky ring

DEEP

passing my tonsils
his long cock slides down my throat
he shoots i savor

ANONYMOUS

alone in the crowd
someone grabs my crotch but who
chaos i can't tell

SPONTANEOUS

we are sexual
lust drives many to their bedrooms
orgasms are quick

GOING OUT

he is in those jeans
my eyes rape his covered crack
let's stay in tonight

SHY

each day that boy smiles
he passes me in the hall
he never says hi

SNEAK PREVIEW

there's his underwear
it creeps out from his loose shorts
he made my morning

PREPPY

he sports his polo
abercrombie obsessive
but on him it works

SMOOTH

my hands roam his chest
drunken laughter then gropes me
his smile travels down

SIX AM

i missed you he says
our lips meet our hands explore
october mornings

TASTE

he is not that big
i don't care while my head bobs
but i love his cream

TEASE

my fingers his waist
tips creep inside his boxers
they brush his soft shaft

CLOSET

he glances over
his eyes filled with guilt and fear
i can still feel them

UNEXPECTED

he touches my leg
waves of passion run through me
a night of pure bliss

FOREPLAY

my teeth his nipples
our thick cocks grind together
my bite finds your nape

LATIN LOCKER ROOM

tight beautiful bod
his brown nipples small hazelnuts
his abs lead the way

SMOOTH

my hands roam his chest
drunk he smiles then grabs my heat
his glasses sink low

BODY BUILD

jocks with socks and briefs
bulges and muscles they sweat
rock hard adonis

FIRST TIME

press into his cleft
resistance then insertion
i love cherry pie

BUSINESS CASUAL

khaki covered crotch
buns wrapped in beige precum stain
hot office fuck toy

STRENGTH

his beautiful curve
his shaft spears upwards arcing
tower of power

SKULLFUCK

push between my lips
slide down my throat push deeper
yeah bro fuck my face

SECRET

when you lift your legs
your secret spot will appear
hungry cave of love

BREAKFAST

sausage and two eggs
then butter and toast those buns
our breakfast in bed

MAN FLESH

chorizo bratwurst
kielbasa pepperoni
boudin andouille

SOAR

magical mattress
soaring shimmering splendid
sideways and under

NINE ONE ONE

what's your problem sir?
some hacker stole my password!
my buttplug won't stop!

BUBBLE BATH

three men in a tub
so soapy and slippery
my kinda party

THICK

layers of flavor
i like men like my bacon
thick cut with pepper

PRE MEANING BEFORE

clear as the first dew
the sweetness, the innocence
tastes just like heaven

WITHIN

so sacred a spot
not very deep but hiding
my pulse of pleasure

STIFLER

he looked back and said
better make that three fingers
i paused to jerk off

BADPUPPY

he's so very bad
so it's the cage or kennel
consistent training

URETHRAL

i'm not into that
i don't like the sound of that
mine's exit only

NIPPLES

such variety
like dimes or pepperonis
sensitive wirings

ORAL IMPULSE

gay queer cocksucker
and i'm better than she is
i am what i eat

COBRA

my hooded serpent
white venom drips from it's fangs
his bite breeds with seed

STRAWBERRY MILK

tasted on his kiss
powder quik from the tin can
my berries and cream

MYRIAD

a kiss can vary much
care love lust and betrayal
our uncertain flesh

PULSE

as you are in me
you hold me as you finish
they lift and tighten

STEADY

i'm glad you asked ace
just three weeks but i'm ready
now raw dog this ass

BLEACH

you don't need all that
listen! your butt looks normal!
all buttholes matter

POST GAME PRO

pro tip to spoil them
super simple and classy
warm damp towelettes

PLAYTIME

just remain silent
your blindfold on, the rope tight
do as Daddy asks

ORIENTAL FLAVOR

cream of sum yung gai
egg rolls and fortune cookies
turning japanese

THE

END

R.A. Lopez grew up with one foot in the 80s
and one in the 90s and still lives most of his life there.
He loves animals but currently only has a fat old ferret
named Fat Ellie, who lost her sister, Tina Tina this year.
He spends a large amount of his time designing worlds
and developing role playing game rules and settings.
He has been writing gaming materials, fiction,
and poetry for over 30 years and blogging for over 25.

His hobbies range all of geekdom from anime to comics,
horror to fantasy, science fiction to video games,
culinary experimentation, philosophy, research,
archiving / blogging about art, media, and politics.
He is a centrist by nature and loves to play devil's advocate.
He is politically an atheist but spiritually keeps his secrets.

His d20 World Setting "Empyrean" and it's companion
adventure module in three parts will be available very soon!
The First Arc "Reality Unbound: Reclaimation"
will be released with the initial release of "Empyrean d20".

R.A. Lopez is also one half of The Moonlight Collection,
a dark and dreamy collaboration of mixed poetry
by two kindred spirits represented by an owl and a pussycat.

Thank You For Purchasing & Reading This Work!
Contact R.A. Lopez @ willworkformoney@hotmail.com

~

Jonathan Rodriguez is an Artist and Illustrator who works
with a variety of mediums and has an eclectic style all his own.
Contact Jonathan Rodriguez @ freelove 6991@yahoo.com

Printed in Great Britain
by Amazon